ACCENTS and REBOUNDS

for the SNARE DRUMMER

George Lawrence Stone's followup book to
STICK CONTROL for the SNARE DRUMMER

By GEORGE LAWRENCE STONE

Nationally Known Authority on Rudimental Drumming
Principal of the Stone Drum and Xylophone School of Boston
and Drum Editor of "The International Musician"

 UPDATED EDITION

©2012 STONE PERCUSSION BOOKS LLC

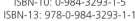 STONE PERCUSSION BOOKS LLC

EXCLUSIVELY DISTRIBUTED BY ALFRED MUSIC PUBLISHING CO., INC.

www.stonepercussionbooks.com   stonepercussionbooks@comcast.net

ISBN-10: 0-984-3293-1-5
ISBN-13: 978-0-984-3293-1-1

Dedicated to

JOE MORELLO

Outstanding Perfectionist in Modern Drumming

Stone Percussion Books LLC, a family company owned by George Lawrence Stone's grandchildren,
would like to thank Dom Famularo for his help and encouragement in the reissue of this and other classic Stone percussion books.
For more information about Dom and his remarkable work in drumming, teaching, publishing,
and motivational workshops and events around the world, visit Dom's website at
www.domfamularo.com

Project Coordinators: Dom Famularo and Joe Bergamini
Layout and engraving: Willie Rose
Text layout: Barbara Haines
Editorial Consultant: Dave Black
Additional help from Steve Forster, Claus Hessler, Stephane Chamberland, and Dave Dieni

Above left: Joe Morello, photo from early edition of *Accents and Rebounds for the Snare Drummer*, courtesy Stone Percussion Books LLC
Above right: Joe Morello later in life, photo by Tony Barbera, courtesy DW Drums
See last page for a list of Joe Morello's publications.

PREFACE

ACCENTS AND REBOUNDS is an advanced textbook designed to follow and reinforce the author's previous book, STICK CONTROL, so widely known and used.

It is presented at the solicitation of (1) the many leading instructors who, having used the former book with such gratifying results, ask for material to follow and (2) the many "name" drummers who consider their daily workout with STICK CONTROL a *must,* and who likewise suggest more of the same.

Accents in varying degrees play an important part in music. Modern music calls more and more for an infinite variety of emphasis. The drums, from their very nature, possess a potential for accentuation far greater than any other musical instrument. Hence, the drummer is looked to above all others for the utmost in dynamics.

The accent routines have been carefully selected from the author's private collection of hand-conditioners and will, with faithful practice, further two-handed dexterity and develop not only the *control* but the *finesse* to meet today's most exacting requirements.

ACCENTS AND REBOUNDS also presents, for the first time, a progressive approach to control of the secondary beat of the roll, so important in the finished execution of this, the drummer's long tone. The routines here are the result of years of study in roll production, and were employed by the author in his private teaching most successfully.

The routines in which accents and rebounds are combined are particularly adaptable to the development of FINGER BOUNCE EXECUTION, a style so effective in modern soloing, in which at speedy tempos sticks are manipulated mainly by finger action.

A special chapter is included on THE BUZZ ROLL in which its relationship to the pure two-beat is spelled out and its use in modern drumming justified.

Study of STICK CONTROL is recommended first, followed by ACCENTS AND REBOUNDS. Regular practice is, of course, a necessity and to the student, the author urges the services of a local expert instructor whenever available.

Boston, Massachusetts   GEORGE LAWRENCE STONE

My studies with Joe Morello had a profound affect on my drumming sound, flexibility, and speed, and I am eternally grateful to have spent so much time with Joe. Almost every exercise and idea Joe showed me required work, but made sense immediately and yielded rapid results. After a couple of months of working with his teacher George L. Stone's book *Stick Control*, Joe introduced me to Stone's *Accents and Rebounds* and to the concepts of up and down strokes, and of controlling stick heights, which Stone had taught him. This was the one idea that I didn't immediately understand or see value in—I struggled with the specific choreography *Accents and Rebounds* required me to master. Of course, I was awed by Joe's facility and musicianship, trusted his judgment and guidance, and so I stuck with it. In time, the exercises in *Accents and Rebounds* began to flow and the choreography, which had previously been slowing me down, began to infect my movements with a new kind of super efficiency. Mastering up and down strokes in the full, half and tap positions was trying but definitely a game-changing moment in my development. I am happy to see the release of this new edition of *Accents and Rebounds* and hope drummers today will take the time to understand and benefit from Stone's concepts.

JOHN RILEY

What you are about to experience with *Accents and Rebounds* is the most natural, effective and efficient movement for drumming. George L. Stone was a master . . . and he got the best performance from his many students, such as Joe Morello, Vic Firth, Buddy Rich, Gene Krupa, and many others. Joe Morello studied with Stone for many years and the "Stone/Morello accent code" was unleashed! Joe's dedication to music and technique is unmatched in drumset performance. I studied with Joe for many years, and he always talked about the advantage to understanding stick movement. This is about up strokes and down strokes, also often called pullouts (low tap to an accent) and control strokes (accent then low tap). Follow the arrows above the measures to see where the stick should be for easier execution. This makes the biggest difference in having total freedom to play what is in your head and heart—immediately! Stone's *Stick Control* gives drummers more control and accuracy. *Accents and Rebounds* then puts the control into dynamic expressive motion. Both books are needed for the complete picture. After more than fifty years, *Accents and Rebounds* is now more relevant than ever for the twenty-first century. Music is always changing, but the fundamentals of movement will remain the same. This book will assist you in achieving a higher understanding of skill and musical expression! George L. Stone lives on in all drummers worldwide!

DOM FAMULARO

QUICK START for this edition of *Accents and Rebounds for the Snare Drummer*

Students and teachers have found *Accents and Rebounds for the Snare Drummer* useful as an advanced followup to *Stick Control for the Snare Drummer*, but even instructors have sometimes been unsure of how best to use the material. Stone assumed that with the guidance of a teacher, students would benefit from the need to analyze the exercises themselves. In this edition we've made an effort to graphically show the techniques.

Up and down arrows	=	**Full stroke (stay up)**
Dash	=	**Tap**
Down arrow	=	**Down stroke**
Up arrow	=	**Up stroke**

We encourage you to start with *Stick Control for the Snare Drummer* and after that to work with a good local teacher, as Stone recommended, to get the most out of this book.

Accents and Rebounds Study Guide

When *Accents and Rebounds* was first produced, there was no mention of the specific techniques to be used when playing the accented notes. Joe Morello, our friend, mentor, and teacher, suggested that it would have been too difficult to describe the methods in print, and that Mr. Stone wanted to allow flexibility in the ways teachers and students would be able to work with the book.

With the availability of instructional DVDs to supplement the following descriptions, these techniques can readily be understood. While they may not be the only approach to playing, they work. Please use the following explanations as a basic study guide, and visit the Stone website at www.stonepercussionbooks.com for more detailed instructions.

The Level System:

The premise behind this method is a simple one: a louder note can be produced by having the drumstick starting from a position which is farther, rather than closer, to the drumhead, allowing the stick to develop enough speed to produce a loud sound—the faster the speed, the louder the tone. If a drum is struck from a low position, a softer sound can be produced.

Free Strokes are strokes that begin at one position and rebound back to the same position. To play a *Full Stroke*, start with the stick straight up and down, with the tip pointing to the ceiling, about 18" from the drum. Strike the drum or pad, accepting the rebound and allowing the stick to return to the starting position. The Full Stroke will do three things: Loosen the muscles, provide for consistent sound, and develop reflexes (your hand must return as fast as the stick does). A *Half Stroke* will start and finish about 9" from the drum, and a *Lower Stroke*, about 3".

Controlled Strokes are combinations of the three Free Strokes and are used to prepare for accenting. The *Down Stroke* will start at the same place a Full Stroke does, but the stick is stopped from rebounding all the way back up, stopping at the half-stroke position, in readiness to play a softer sound. The *Up Stroke* is the opposite of a *Down Stroke*, starting from a low position and going to a higher one, in preparation to play a loud or accented note. A Down Stroke will be used for playing an accent when the following note to be played is unaccented. An Up Stroke will be used when the next note played is accented. For example, Down Strokes may be played 18" to 9", 18" to 3" or 9" to 3". Up strokes are played 9" to 18", 3" to 18" or 3" to 9". For example, if four loud strokes were to be played followed by four soft strokes, you would play:

FULL, FULL, DOWN, DOWN, TAP, TAP, UP, UP

Paradiddles with an accent on the beat would be:

DOWN, UP, TAP TAP, DOWN, UP, TAP TAP
(also called DUTT, DUTT)

Practicing the exercises in this book, and if necessary writing down under the exercises F. D, U, or T, will enable the serious student the flexibility to play accented patterns in a variety of stickings with ease.

Practice slowly at first. Avoid tension.
Precision plus accuracy equals control.
Control plus endurance equals speed.

DANNY GOTTLIEB and STEVE FORSTER

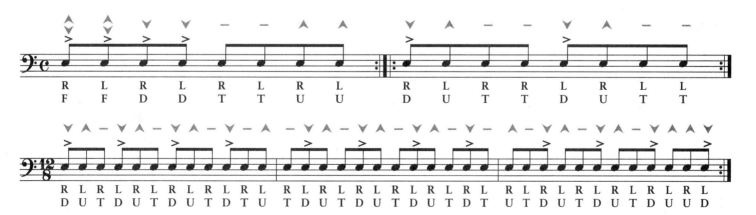

Accented Eighths

Repeat each exercise twenty times or more before playing the final ending.

Accented Eighths

Accent heavily in practice—lighter in actual playing.

Accented Eighths

Accented Eighths

Accented Dotted Notes

* Practice using the legitimate dotted rhythm as shown above,
  but also in the modern (loose) interpretation of jazz:

Accented Dotted Notes

Accent heavily in practice—lighter in actual playing.

Accented Dotted Notes

Also practice in the interpretation of jazz:

Accented Dotted Notes

Accented Triplets

Repeat each exercise twenty times or more before playing the final ending.

Accented Triplets

Accent heavily in practice—lighter in actual playing.

Accented Triplets

Accented Triplets

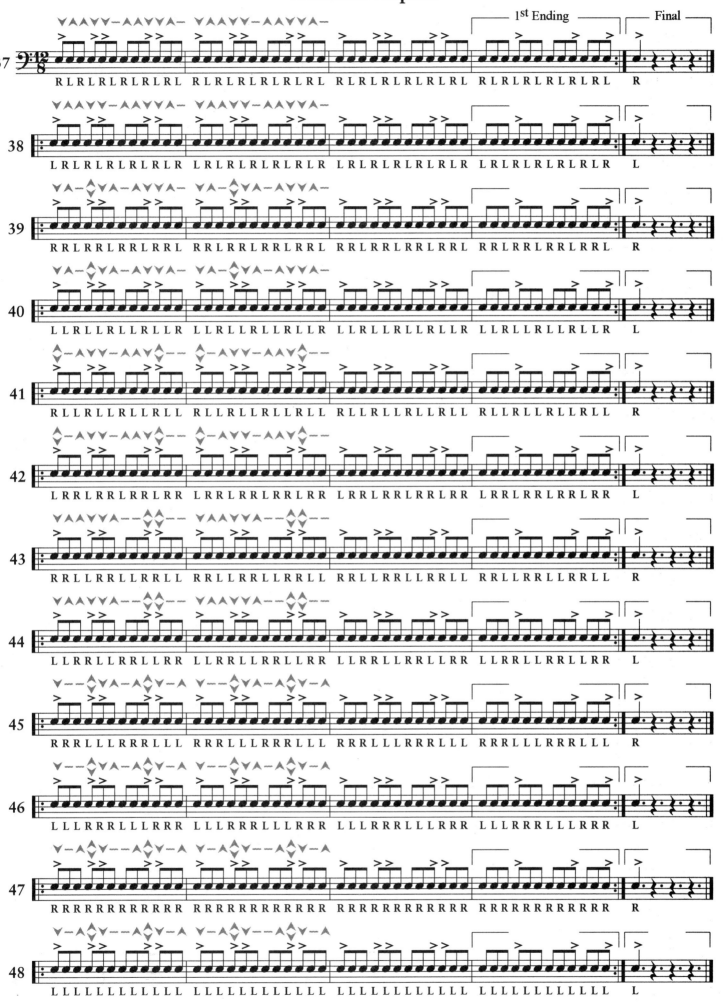

REBOUND CONTROL (for the Two-Beat Roll)

That age-old cliché *A chain is only as strong as its weakest link* could be paraphrased thus: *The drummer's roll is only as smooth as its secondary beat.*

It is impossible to produce a "perfect" roll on a drum because, while the initial roll-beat of either stick is struck by hand (or finger) action, the following (the secondary) beat must be produced by rebounding—by bounce.

The bouncing of a drumstick may be compared with that of a rubber ball. In bouncing the ball to the floor, its initial impact produces a blow of given power, but the rebounds which follow strike with correspondingly less power, one by one, until the ball finally comes to rest.

The same principle applies to the rebounding of the sticks. Indeed, if with either sticks or ball we could make rebounds (one or more) as strong in power as the initial impact, the sticks would rebound to perfection, the ball would bounce forever, and we would have discovered the secret of perpetual motion.

Hence, there must always be a certain degree of irregularity in power between our initial roll-beat and its rebound.

The following routines, in which rebounds often appear and are accented *on the beat*, are designed to develop maximum control of rebounds to the extent that our rolls will, at least to the ear, most closely approximate "perfection."   GLS

Slow, even tempos first, striking both roll-beats by individual hand action
Faster speeds later, now rebounding, up to capacity

REBOUND CONTROL (for the Two-Beat Roll)

Accent heavily in practice. Do not buzz in these exercises.

REBOUND CONTROL (for the Two-Beat Roll)

Follow the numbers.

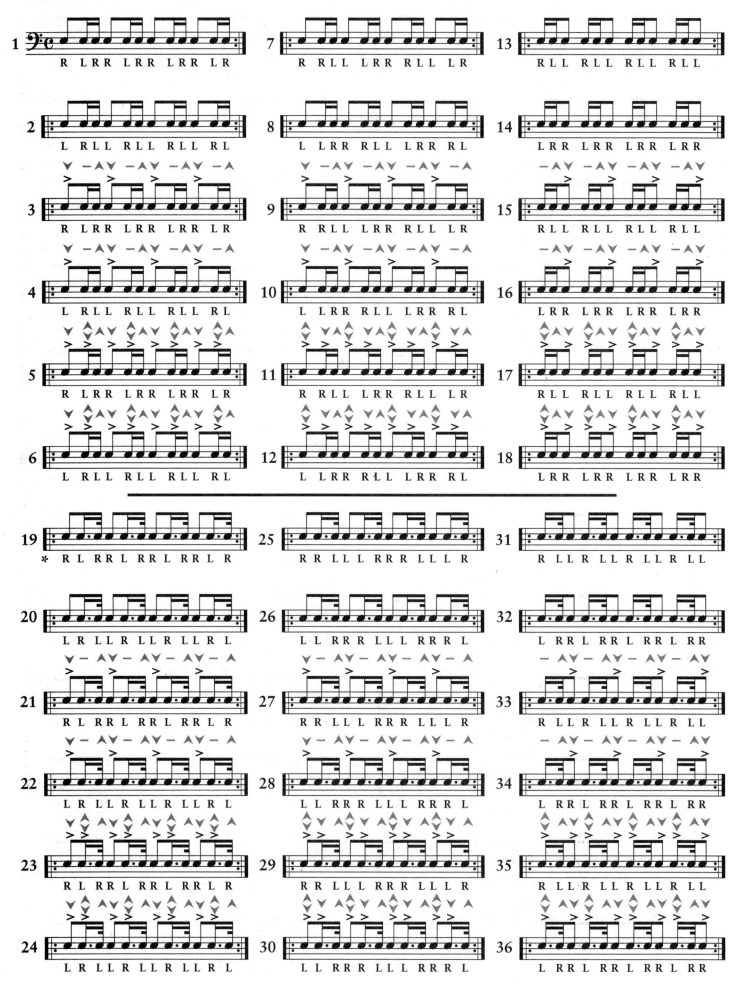

* Also practice using this jazz rhythm:

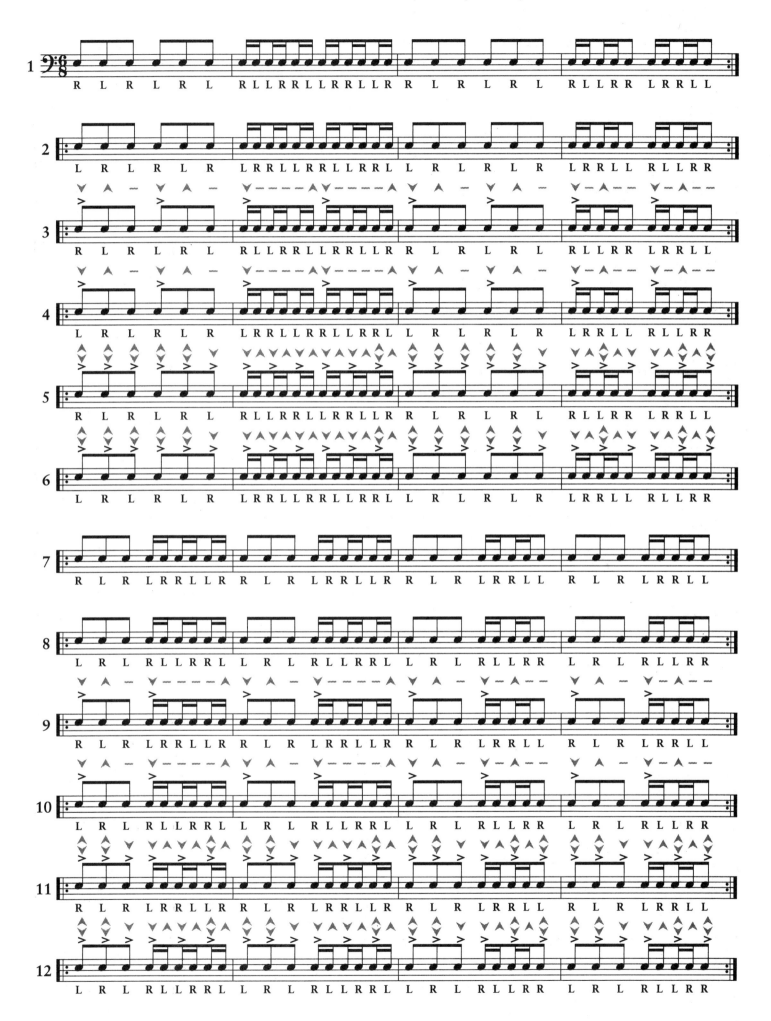

REBOUND CONTROL (in 5/8)

(in 7/8)

REBOUND CONTROL (in the Four-Stroke Ruff)

The grace notes here are most effectively executed by finger-bounce action.

REBOUND CONTROL – A (in Triplets and Dots)

* In the jazz idiom, more often played as:

REBOUND CONTROL – B (in Triplets and Dots)

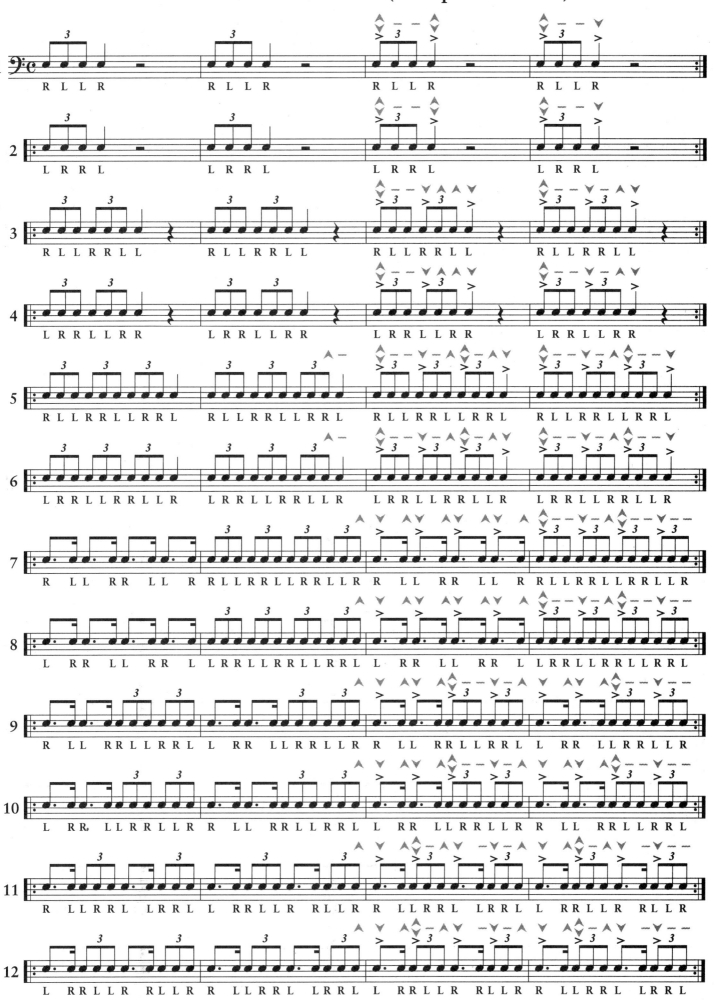

THE TWO-BEAT ROLL is the pure roll and consists of two beats with either stick; the first beat struck, the second beat rebounded (bounced).

THE BUZZ ROLL consists of more than two beats with either stick.

A BEAT AND REBOUND OF EITHER STICK

A BUZZ OF EITHER STICK

WHEREAS A SLIGHT DOWNWARD PRESSURE OF HANDS AND FINGERS as a stick strikes its initial beat produces the single rebound of the TWO-BEAT ROLL, a further downward pressure will give two, three, or more rebounds, thus producing the BUZZ.   GLS

(Reprinted by permission from the author's TECHNIQUE ON PERCUSSION in International Musician.)

THE TWO-BEAT ROLL VERSUS THE BUZZ

The buzz roll has ever been a controversial subject among drummers, mainly because its character, uses and limitations have not fully been understood.

Prejudice against it apparently started in early war times with the inception of military drumming, in which the drummer's duties were confined to outdoor drumming for marching soldiers.

The rolls, then employed on a giant parade drum with heavy drumsticks were, perforce, powerful in nature, and here buzzing was definitely out of place. Hence, our drummer of this era was warned against buzzing, and he in turn transmitted this warning to those who followed.

THEN AND NOW

Through the intervening years, new developments in music and in drumming have come into existence one-by-one. New and different instruments have been introduced into our percussion section. These, in themselves, have called for innovations, new techniques; and one of the latter has been the buzzing of the roll.

For many years the author in his teaching, magazine articles and in clinics, has endeavored to emphasize the importance of the buzz (sometimes called *press* or *crush*) roll and justify its use in our drumming of today. Why? Because it is a natural extension of our traditional two-beat roll. Because it represents an additional tool of the drumming trade, not merely a *good enough* or *get by* device to replace the two-beat.

ROLLS VERSUS SANDPAPER

Today, the all-round drummer finds use for as many degrees of coarseness and fineness in his rolls as there are in sandpaper, each degree dedicated to its particular purpose and type of drum. While it is agreed that the pure two-beat roll comes first in rudimental importance and still is the preferred roll of the stylist, modern drumming, especially on a small wire-snared drum played with lightweight sticks, more often calls for a finer, smoother roll, aptly said to resemble "the patter of raindrops on a tin roof" or the "the tearing of a piece of silk cloth."

Wire snares buzz by themselves at the slightest sound disturbance or the single tap of a stick. Indeed they often buzz by remote control, i.e., at certain tones played on some nearby wind instrument. Hence it is difficult, even while attempting a two-beat roll on the sensitive wire-snared drum, to achieve anything but a buzz, for the snares move faster than the sticks.

"AVOID THE BUZZ" IS FOR THE BEGINNER

Yes, many fine teachers tell their students to *avoid the buzz*. The writer believes this admonition to be a good one, but such a warning is primarily intended for *practice* and particularly, *for the beginner*, so that he may be trained to master the more difficult but more generally accepted two-beat roll first.

Later, as training and experience develop the talents of the beginner (or indeed any seeker for more proficiency), he will find control of his rolls developing alongside; his ultimate objective being the ability to apply them in their many gradations of tone, from the *pianissimo* of the soft and fine buzz on the smaller drum to the *fortissimo* roar of the two-beat, played on the gut-snared military drum.

IT IS HERE, WITHIN THE SOUND-SCOPE OF THE ROLL—THE DRUMMER'S LONG TONE—THAT THE BUZZ OCCUPIES ITS HIGHLY IMPORTANT PLACE.

In the following exercises, the execution of one roll is contrasted with that of the other. The object is to develop sensitivity of hands and fingers and through this, a wider range of control and expression in rolling.

Slow practice is indicated first at unvarying tempo, with completely relaxed muscular action. Timing is the most important element here, WITH HANDS MOVING AT THE SAME RATE OF SPEED IN ONE ROLL AS IN THE OTHER. (Avoid the natural tendency to rush the buzzes.)

Note well that in slow tempos the buzzes will suffer, sounding crude and draggy, with spaces in between. However, when in later practice, speed is increased to normal playing tempos, the buzzes in the same exercises will "smooth up" to sound as normal rolls should.

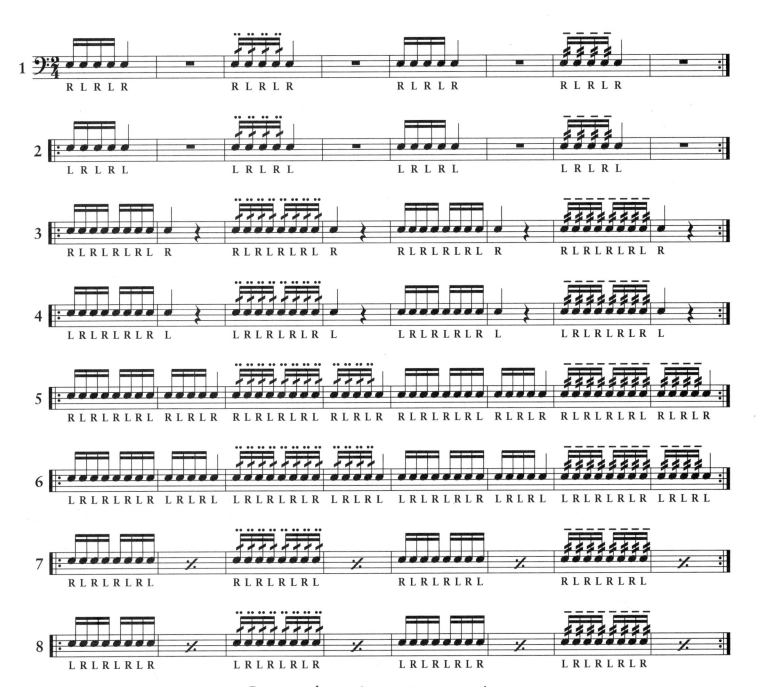

Repeat each exercise twenty or more times.

THE TWO-BEAT ROLL versus THE BUZZ

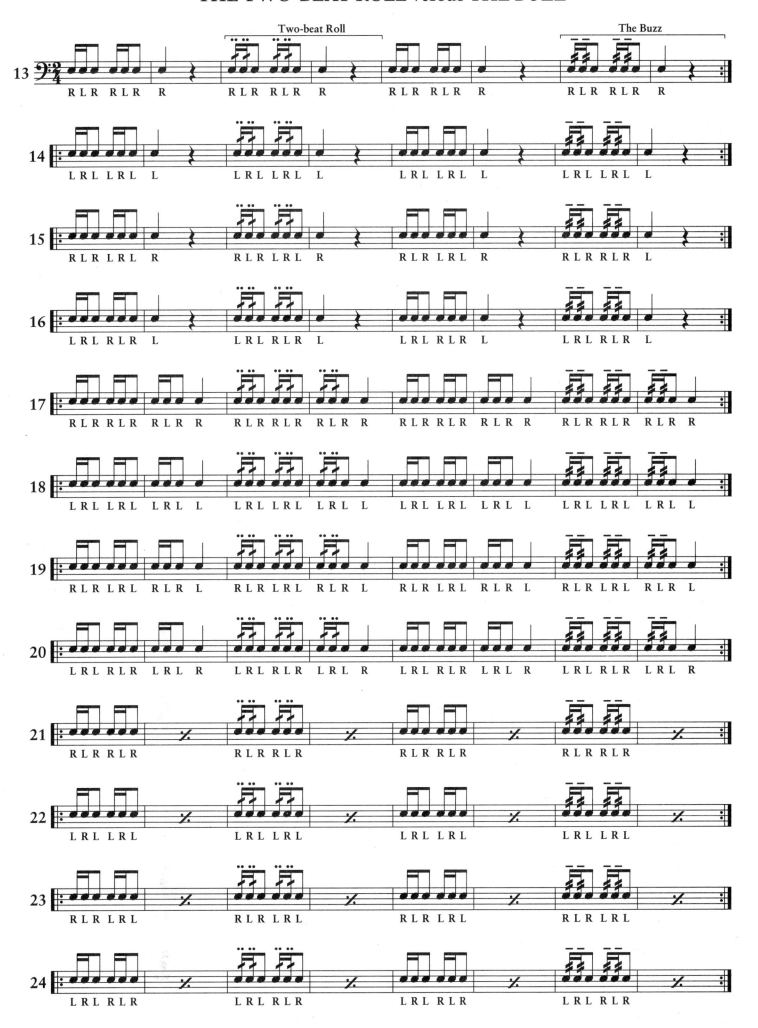

THE TWO-BEAT ROLL versus THE BUZZ

Follow the numbers.

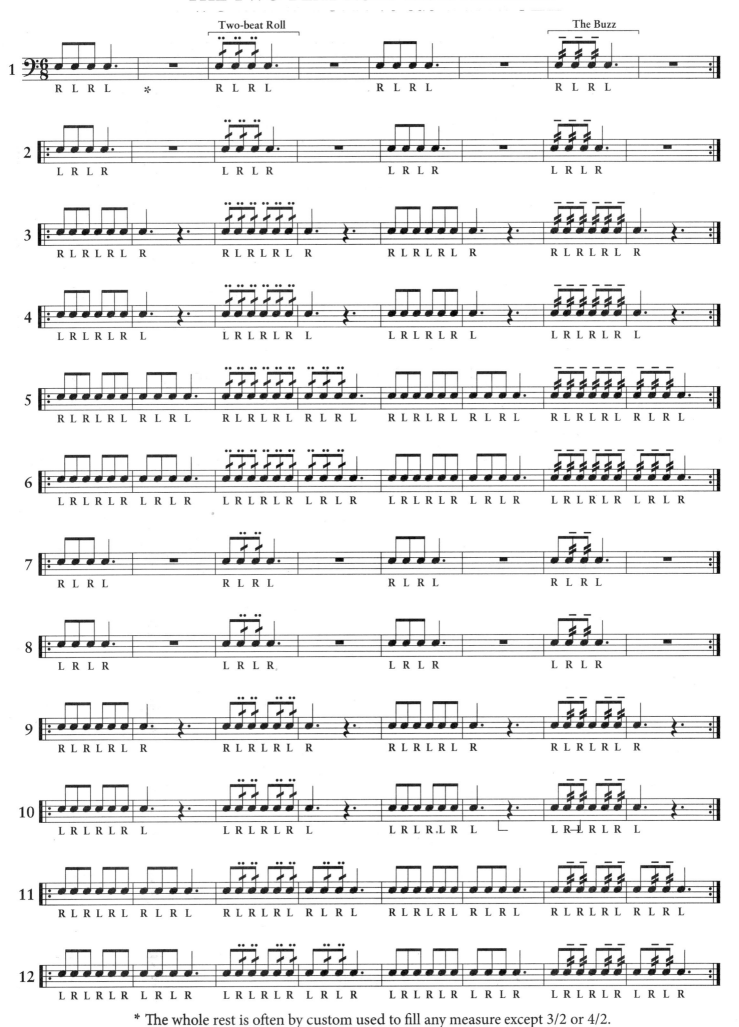

* The whole rest is often by custom used to fill any measure except 3/2 or 4/2.

THE TWO-BEAT ROLL versus THE BUZZ

THE TWO-BEAT ROLL versus THE BUZZ

Follow the numbers.

ACCENTS IN PROGRESSIVE ROLLS (Right Lead)

Slow speeds first, striking both roll-beats (the doubled sixteenths) by individual hand action

Faster speeds later, now rebounding secondary roll-beats, up to capacity

ACCENTS IN PROGRESSIVE ROLLS (Left Lead)

Two-beat roll here. Do not buzz.

ACCENTS IN FIVE-STROKE ROLLS

Slow speeds first, striking both roll-beats (the doubled sixteenths) by individual hand action
Faster speeds later, now rebounding secondary roll-beats, up to capacity

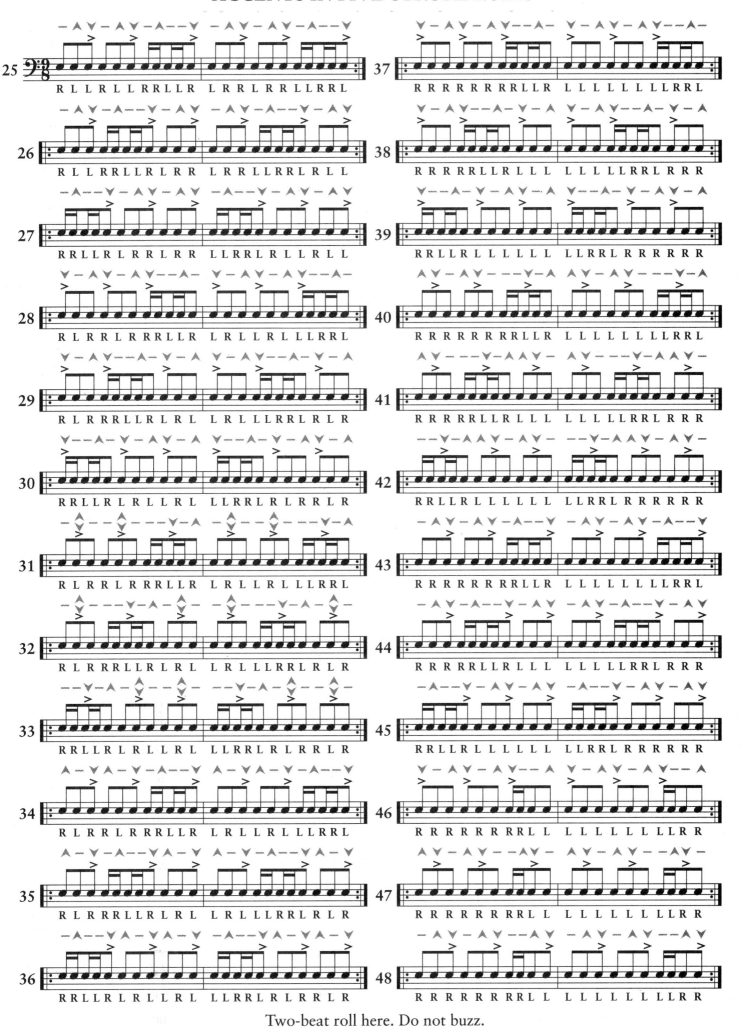

Two-beat roll here. Do not buzz.

ACCENTS IN SEVEN-STROKE ROLLS

ACCENTS IN FIVES AND SEVENS

ROLLING IN MIXED RHYTHM (A)

The Two-beat, not the Buzz, is the preferred roll here.

ROLLING IN MIXED RHYTHM (B)

ROLLING IN MIXED RHYTHM (C)

ROLLING IN MIXED RHYTHM (D)

Works by Joe Morello

Master Studies
Exercises for the Development of Control and Technique
Book from Modern Drummer Publications, Inc.
This is the book on hand development and drumstick control. *Master Studies* focuses on these important aspects: accent studies, buzz-roll exercises, single and double-stroke patterns, control studies, flam patterns, dynamic development, endurance studies, and much more!

Master Studies II
More Exercises for the Development
of Control and Technique
Book from Modern Drummer Publications, Inc.
Like *Master Studies*, this is a workbook of material to use in developing the hands for drumming. Challenging exercises encourage students to learn slow, sensible and accurate practice techniques.

Rudimental Jazz
A Musical Application of Rudiments to the Drumset
Book with CD from Modern Drummer Publications, Inc.
Originally released in 1967, this Joe Morello classic is once again available—now with CD! The precursor to his two most widely used instructional books—*Master Studies* and *Master Studies II*—this book covers: techniques such as right- and left-hand grips, playing position, striking the snare drum and hi-hat and more; beginning exercises; drum beats; teachers' charts; graphic cutouts, and more. Includes a foreword and an introduction.

Joe Morello, Drum Method 1:
The Natural Approach to Technique
DVD from Hot Licks
Joe Morello was one of the most important drummers in jazz, and here is your chance to learn directly from him! Joe demonstrates roll techniques, matched grip and traditional stick positions, sounds on the drumhead, cross sticking, tuning, and much more, all using natural body movement. Plus, great vintage footage of Joe in action with Dave Brubeck Quintet!

Joe Morello, Drum Method 2: Around the Kit
DVD from Hot Licks
Part 2 of Joe's classic drum method series explores single vs. double bass drum techniques, special bass drum exercises, heel-toe techniques, hi-hat "ride style" and "fanning," making hi-hat and cymbals "breathe" and blend, swinging and keeping time, dynamics, punctuating and accents, thinking musically, and soloing. This wealth of practical teaching is accompanied, as ever, by Joe Morello's legendary wit and wisdom!

For bookings apply to
GEORGE LAWRENCE STONE
(Nationally known authority on Rudimental Drumming)
61 Hanover Street   Boston, Mass.
(Tel. CApitol 7454)

Photo from a brochure promoting two of Stone's lectures on music appreciation, c. 1932, courtesy Stone Percussion Books LLC.

**See more of the text of this brochure at
www.stonepercussionbooks.com**

[STONE PERCUSSION BOOKS LLC]

www.stonepercussionbooks.com
stonepercussionbooks@comcast.net